The Civil War Reenactor's

**The Civil War Reenactor's Blackpowder Guide
to the *safe* use, care and maintenance of
Replica Period Firearms**

© Copyright 1998 by David T.T. Smith
Second Printing – September 1999

Published by:

P.O. Box 3574, Gettysburg, PA 17325

All photographs by the author   Design and layout by the author

Printed in U.S.A.

ISBN 0-9663443-0-8

All rights reserved
No part of this book may be reproduced
in any form without written permission from the publisher
except in the form of brief excerpts or quotations for the purposes of review.
Making copies of this book, or any portion of it, for any purpose other than your own is a
violation of United States copyright laws.

*This information should not be taken as a recommendation to hand load
either blank or live ammunition for either antique or replica firearms and
no liability is implied or assumed. After careful inspection of antique firearms
by qualified gunsmiths, the reader must make his own decisions about whether
to load and fire either blank or live blackpowder ammunition. User assumes
all risks, responsibility and liability for any and all injuries, losses and
damages to persons or property arising from use of data found in this book.*

The Civil War Reenactor's Blackpowder Guide

To insure historical accuracy in reenacting attire, *The Civil War Reenactor's Blackpowder Guide* recommends

Timeless Textiles

Which sells silks, wools, linens, brocades and cottons suitable for Civil War era clothing.

Timeless Textiles is located at 110 Mill Street, Suite #9, Middletown, PA 17057
Telephone 717-930-0928   FAX 717-930-0847

Timeless Textiles will be opening a store in the Gettysburg area in the near future.

The Civil War Reenactor's Blackpowder Guide

Acknowledgments

Primary thanks go to Dana Heim, who first welcomed me to Civil War reenacting and then asked me to accept a most difficult and sometimes thankless job, that of Safety Officer for our United States Volunteers Civil War Reenactment Brigade, for his encouragement and kind endorsement commentary on my book. Over four long years, all of us have made great strides in making our hobby a safer place to be.

Thanks also to Reg Wirth, Aide-in-Charge of the USV, for his ongoing advice and critique as this book took shape.

A big thank-you also goes to Bill and Mona Raymond of the USV's 2d US Cavalry for their expert help in equestrian matters and for their kind assistance with and loan of firearms for some of the photography, as well as reviewing drafts of this book.

Thanks also to Craig Beachler, USV Cavalry Chief and commander of the 2d US Cavalry for his comments and advice on practical field related maintenance issues with the carbine and revolver.

Thanks to Mike Roberts of the USV's 56th New York Volunteer Infantry for his invaluable help on the field as a safety officer at many events and also for sharing his practical knowledge gained through his many years of experience as a reenactor. He and I together experienced blown musket nipples first hand on the field and then, as we investigated further trying to find the cause, opened the "Pandora's Box" of nipple threads, which resulted in Appendix 1.

Thank you to the folks at Navy Arms who were kind enough to allow me the run of their place and to photograph several of their stock Civil War replica firearms for inclusion in this work.

Thanks to George Lomas of The Regimental Quartermaster and his brother Gene for their assistance in tracking down nipple specifications.

Special thanks to Sue Hawkins and Tammy Loy of Taylor & Co, importers of Armi-Sport, who particularly went out of their way to help and thanks also to Euroarms of America both of whom kindly provided me with information on nipple sizes for all of their products which very important data which is included in this book.

Last, but certainly not least, a heartfelt thank you to my many friends in the reenactment hobby of both blue and gray and all branches of service, all of whom would take a chapter to list, for their ongoing assistance in many innumerable ways, both on and off the field.

The Civil War Reenactor's Blackpowder Guide

Table of Contents

Acknowledgements	iii
Introduction	2
Chapter 1 - Choosing Equipment and other basics	3
Chapter 2 - School of the Musket	8
Chapter 3 - School of the Carbine	16
Chapter 4 - School of the Revolver	22
Chapter 5 - Specialty Replica Firearms	37
Appendix 1 - Nipple Grid	46
Appendix 2 - Blackpowder Substitutes	51
Glossary	52

The Civil War Reenactor's Blackpowder Guide

Introduction

This book was conceived after observing first hand the lack of, and distinct need for, written instructions on proper loading, cleaning, maintenance *and safe useage* of various Civil War era replica black powder firearms as used today by thousands of Civil War reenactors. Many excellent, comprehensive books have been written on live shooting of black powder replica fireams. However, virtually nothing has been written about the safe and proper methodology of loading and firing of blank rounds in reenactments.

Many reenactors simply join a unit and purchase equipment without a clear knowledge of how properly to load and fire other than following the lead of the next soldier in line. Some units assign an experienced NCO as a mentor for their "fresh fish" and some do not. Some units have written procedures for safe handling and firing and others do not.

This book will provide clear guidance for both the beginning and veteran reenactor alike that will ensure correct and safe useage of Civil War era black powder replica firearms and will hopefully result in making our wonderful hobby more enjoyable and safer for many years to come.

Every Civil War reenactment unit should recommend that each new unit member purchase a copy of this book for his or her personal own use as that reenactor begins to acquire equipment.

The Civil War Reenactor's Blackpowder Guide

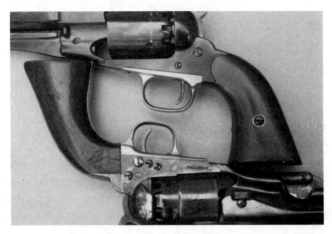

Chapter 1 Choosing Equipment and other basics

Many reenactors unfortunately become victims of instant gratification and spur of the moment decisions when making purchasing decisions that will have long-term ramifications. It is wise to remember that thought, research and care put into the purchase of Civil War replica firearms will serve the reenactor well through the many years of his or her "career" in the hobby. Unit commanders should make it a standard practice to assign a veteran to each "fresh fish" not only to help with drill, but also to accompany the new reenactor to advise on firearm selection.

The watchword here is quality. Most Civil War era replica firearms are reasonably good arms and will serve the reenactor well through many years of hard service. Differences, however, will be found in fit and finish of the parts, precision in the lockwork and other fine points in higher quality arms. The extra time and effort put into finding and selecting exactly the right arm or arms of the quality you desire for your intended purpose may save you money and aggravation over the long haul.

Most Civil War reenactment units will only allow a three banded musket for infantry use, usually an Enfield Model 1853 replica or Springfield replica of either the 1861 or 1863 model. Some reenactors prefer to use the Springfield Model 1842 .69 caliber percussion smoothbore musket replica, which is also a three banded musket. This is not an historic requirement as many 2 banded muskets were used in the Civil War, but is a practical and safety related requirement. A three banded musket has a long enough barrel (usually 40" as opposed to 33" for a two bander) so that the rear rank soldier can safely fire with the barrel over his first rank filemate's shoulder. This is safely done by keeping the first rank soldier's shoulder in between the rear and middle barrel bands (those closest to the lock mechanism). This "first and second band rule" insures that neither the muzzle nor the percussion cap come too close to the first rank soldier's ear. Some reenactors either wear ear plugs or use a bit of cotton as their Civil War ancestors did as an extra measure of hearing protection.

The Civil War Reenactor's Blackpowder Guide

Cavalry and artillery units that use two banded muskets or musketoons should refer to the chapter on muskets.

Use of Original Firearms

There are many fine quality original rifles, carbines and pistols available from the 1861 - 1865 era. Many people today still enjoy firing these originals as a part of their "Civil War experience".

The steels used in originals, however, do not approach the quality of those used in modern replica black powder firearms, and, as a result, many reenactors choose not to use original firearms in reenactments. Some events sponsors simply prohibit use of originals outright usually because their liability insurer will not allow them.

Any reenactor wishing to use an original firearm should have the piece inspected by a competent gunsmith (and preferably magna fluxed or X rayed to uncover any hidden defects or cracks in the gunmetal). The reenactor should be sure to check with event sponsors to be sure that originals are allowed. Another important factor to be considered is that continued firing of an original firearm will almost certainly reduce its value as a collectible.

All nipples are _not_ created equal.

Actually, there is quite a bit more to a nipple (or cone as it was referred to in the 1860's) than meets the eye. The nipple is that essential part of the percussion firearm which conveys the flash from the percussion cap either directly to the powder in each chamber of the revolver or to the flash channel and then to the powder in the combustion chamber of the musket and carbine.

It is absolutely essential that the reenactor learn exactly which nipple his musket, carbine or revolver uses. Otherwise, there is the very real danger of installing a miss-fitted or cross threaded nipple which could blow out of the nipple hole on firing with potentially harmful results. There is more discussion of this issue in each chapter on the different types of firearms and also a comprehensive chart in Appendix 1 showing what types of nipples are supplied in most of the replica firearms used in Civil War reenacting today.

Regardless of the type or types of firearms you are working with, *you must remember that all nipples are not manufactured to the same specifications*, i.e., different manufacturers utilize different threads. Some manufacturers even use different types of threads from one model to the other, or astonishingly, different nipples on the same models that are manufactured for different distributors. Sound confusing? It can be unless you know how to identify which nipple your firearm uses. Most musket, carbine and revolver nipple threads are manufactured to one of several industry standards. They are as follows:

The Civil War Reenactor's Blackpowder Guide

1) National Course Thread is also known as United States Standard (USS). These threads are usually expressed in inches of diameter or fractions thereof and in threads per inch (TPI). An example would be 5/16" diameter x 20 TPI as used by the Euroarms Enfield rifle-musket imported by Dixie Gun Works.

2) National Fine Thread is also known as Society of Automotive Engineering (SAE). These are expressed with a nominal, arbitrary diameter number and in threads per inch (TPI). An example would be a diameter of 12 x 24 TPI, as used in the Ruger Old Army percussion revolver.

3) Metric. These are expressed in metric diameter and in "pitch" or distance between threads. For example, 5.5mm x .9mm as used in the Uberti 1851 Navy revolver.

Thread gauges are inexpensive and readily available from sources such as Sears & Roebuck, Dixie Gun Works, Brownell's and many other well stocked automotive and firearm distributors. *Every reenactment unit should have at least one set of thread gauges both in inch & metric measurement and should be actively using them to check their members' muskets to ensure that the right nipple is in use <u>in each and every musket in the unit!</u>* Better yet, buy one yourself as part of your reenactment kit!

Rollin' yer own paper cartridges?

There are as many varieties of, and methods for, rolling paper musket cartridges as there are reenactors. Suffice it to say that a paper tube, of sufficient size to safely hold at least 60 grains of black powder, either purchased from a sutler or rolled by the reenactor forms the basis for the cartridge. One may also buy pre-rolled cartridges packed complete with percussion caps, also wrapped in paper. All similarity ends there, however, as there will be found an endless variety of methods for folding and securing the end of the paper. Some reenactors, cavalry troopers in particular, prefer paper "tails" with which to grasp the cartridge for removal from the cartridge box and insertion into the carbine breech. Make them up whatever way works best for you to have a safe, smooth load. *If you buy pre-packaged paper cartridges, be sure to immediately separate the wrapped percussion caps from the cartridges. There have been reports of live percussion caps being mistakenly loaded down the bore of a musket.*

Blackpowder blank rounds are extremely dangerous at close range

Anyone who wonders why reenactors elevate their muskets when firing at close range need only conduct his own experiment to see why. Take an old bed sheet and hang it from the limb of a tree. Load your musket with a 60 grain blank charge and back off ten feet. Aim at the center of the sheet and fire. The size of the hole will surprise you!

The Civil War Reenactor's Blackpowder Guide

Powder granulations

There are four different granulations of black powder available today on the market. The essential difference between the grades is the size of the powder granules and hence the speed with which the powder burns.

The first, FG or 1F cannon grade is not suitable for, and should never be used in small arms.

FFG or 2F is the granulation normally used for blackpowder rifles in live fire. Some reenactment units find that FFG is suitable for their use for rifle blanks.

FFFG or 3F, probably the most widely used grade of powder in reenacting, is normally used in revolvers both for live fire and blank rounds, and is also suitable for and widely used in the reenactment community for rifle blank cartridges as well.

FFFFG or 4F is a very fine granulation powder and is only suitable for use in flash pans of flintlocks and therefore not used in the Civil War reenactment hobby. Using 4F in any percussion firearm as a main charge could be dangerous due to its fast burn rate.

Black Powder Equivalents, Substitutes and Replacements

There are several other types of "black powder substitutes" on the market today. Most of them have very limited usefulness in reenacting, mainly because they must be compressed for optimum performance. Since these substitutes are generally not used in reeenacting, we will limit our discussion of these uses to the Appendix. *Under no circumstances should smokeless powder be used in any blackpowder firearm!!*

Percussion Caps

There is only one size cap for use on muskets and carbines - the standard "winged" cap which is available from a variety of sources. In some limited applications, such as cavalry, a reenactor may wish to replace the carbine nipple with one that uses pistol caps so that only one type of cap need be carried.

There is a bit more variety in percussion caps available for revolvers. The "standard" size is the #11 cap which can be used on just about all types of revolvers, albeit with a little bit of "help" such as a slight squeeze to keep the cap from sliding off the nipple.

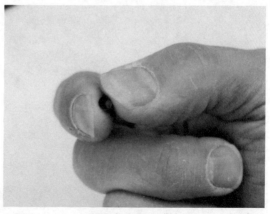

A slight squeeze will help keep a #11 cap on a revolver nipple.

The Civil War Reenactor's Blackpowder Guide

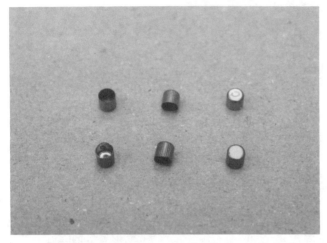

A #10 percussion cap is also available. It is slightly smaller than the #11 and more suitable for pieces such as the 1849 Pocket and the 1862 Pocket Police, which have tighter clearances between the frame and cylinder due to their smaller size. For purposes of our discussion, however, the #10 or #11 either will work well with the Remington 1858, the Colt 1851 Navy or 1860 Army.

#11 caps are in the top row and #10 caps on the bottom.

The Civil War Reenactor's Blackpowder Guide

Chapter 2   School of the Musket

This chapter and the subsequent chapters on the carbine and revolver are not "school" in the sense of Hardee's or Casey's, "by the numbers" but instead offer a practical guide and many useful tips gained by experience with these arms in the reenactment hobby.

Prior to loading

Any time you pick up a firearm, it should be checked to be sure it is clear, that is unloaded and therefore safe to handle. Clearing a musket should consist of insuring that there is neither a live cap on the nipple nor a charge in the bore. Once you are sure your musket is clear, then proceed further. Regardless of whether you fired your musket last week or last year, check your musket barrel for obstructions or debris. When you remove your tompion *put it in your tent and leave it there for the duration of the event!* Inadvertently placed in the bore after loading, a tompion can become a deadly projectile. Better yet, leave your tompion at home! It is not an essential piece of equipment.

Enfield Rifle Tompion

Inverting your musket will allow any loose stuff to fall out of the muzzle such as pieces of straw from the last event. Or maybe you lost a patch down there when you last cleaned it. Even worse, maybe a piece of gravel (a potential projectile) is still there from when you grounded arms at the last event. In any event, give your musket a quick shake with the muzzle down and give the breech a sharp rap with the flat of your hand to dislodge any "stuff" that may be in the bore.

The Civil War Reenactor's Blackpowder Guide

Then draw your ramrod, *(this is the only time other than during arms inspection, in demonstrations and in cleaning that a ramrod should be used, as it too, can become a deadly projectile)* insert it with the "jag" or "button" end first **(1)**, and gently allow it to slide down the bore as you would (and will do later at your unit's safety inspection prior to marching in the day's battle) at inspection arms. Be sure to lower it gently as dropping it even when it is partially inserted in the bore can dent or damage your musket's breech plug or even worse, the breech if you have a solid, one piece barrel. When the end strikes the breech, it should make a sharp "cling". If not, the musket is either dirty or there is something in the bore that must come out before the musket can be fired.

If you fire your musket "live", be sure to check for lead ring buildup at the base of the barrel by probing with your ramrod. This is caused by the explosion of the powder charge melting a minuscule portion of the base of the skirt on each minie ball fired which then adheres to the breech area resulting in a lead ring building up. This lead ring will cause the ramrod to "bump" toward the center of the bore when it is moved slowly up the barrel with the inserted end pressed against the barrel. A bore light which will reach to the breech area is another way to check for lead ring buildup. **Any musket which has or is suspected to have a lead ring built up in the breech cannot be used in an event as the lead ring can become a projectile!** If you do shoot live regularly, you may want to consider keeping an extra barrel or even have a musket specifically for live shooting that you do not bring to reenactments.

Why all this fuss now, you may think. After all, my unit is going to conduct a safety inspection anyway. But, wouldn't it be better to discover any problems *now* so that you can correct them before the scheduled battle? After all, did you drive all these miles to this event only to find that your musket is unserviceable and that you can't participate in the battle? Certainly not! That's why every reenactor should do his own safety inspection *before* his unit does.

If your musket is simply dirty, then your ramrod should go all the way to the bottom of the bore and should only protrude about 1/4" above the muzzle, or to the extent of the threads on the end of the ramrod. If your musket's dirty, then shame on you! Your musket should have been cleaned after your last event. Hopefully, the rust won't be too bad and you can clean it up in time for the day's fight.

If your ramrod protrudes further than this, check for barrel obstructions.

However, if the ramrod is sticking up further, then there is definitely something in the bore and it must come out before you can load or fire. The first corrective action to be

9

The Civil War Reenactor's Blackpowder Guide

taken is a worm on the threaded end of your ramrod. Hopefully, that will remove the offending debris. *Be sure that the worm is not left in the barrel!* If that measure fails, then the breech plug of the gun must come off to gain access. Unfortunately, this will put you out of action for the weekend, as either a breech plug removal or removal of debris from a musket with a solid barrel will require the services of a competent gunsmith.

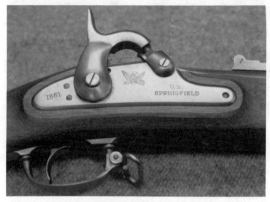

1861 Springfield Cleanout Screw

If your musket passes the "ramrod test," the next step is to inspect the nipple and the bolster area. 1861 Springfields and some others have a "cleanout" screw which, when removed, allows access to the combustion chamber. Using a good quality screwdriver of the proper size, check and make sure that this screw is tight. If you have an Enfield or 1863 Springfield, the bolster does not have a cleanout screw.

Next, take your nipple wrench and insure that your nipple is properly threaded into the bolster. If the nipple does not bottom out or if the threads seem exceptionally tight part way in, this could be the symptom of a threading problem and the musket should not be loaded or fired until you are sure the nipple is properly seated. There have been isolated instances reported of musket nipples blowing out of bolsters on firing, creating a serious and potentially deadly safety hazard.

Note that nipple is *not fully seated!*

A thread gauge will insure that you are using the correct nipple.

If the nipple seems to be too loose or too tight, check (see Appendix 1) proper threads for replica muskets. A thread gauge will tell you if the nipple is correct. If it is not, replace the nipple with the proper one. If the problem still persists, *do not attempt to fire the musket! Take it to a competent gunsmith for repair.* A blown nipple becomes a projectile, which, after ricocheting off the hammer face, **can kill or badly injure the reenactor in the front rank!**

The Civil War Reenactor's Blackpowder Guide

Once you are sure that the bore is clear and the nipple is tight, check the nipple itself for obstructions with a nipple pick. The musket hammer face should then be inspected to insure an even strike on the nipple. A solid circle indicates a solid strike where a crescent or figure-eight mark indicates an off-center strike, which could possibly result in percussion cap fragments breaking off on firing, <u>creating a severe hazard to the eyes!</u> If you are in any doubt about whether your musket is safe to fire, do not attempt to fire it! Have it checked over by a competent gunsmith as soon as possible. Once you are sure your hammer strike is correct, prime the piece and, after informing your pards that you are about to test-fire, place the muzzle in front of a blade of grass or a leaf and fire. The explosion of the cap should move the leaf, indicating that the bore is clear. Your musket should now "pass muster" at your unit's safety inspection and is ready to be loaded. Be sure to *leave the spent percussion cap on the musket nipple!* More on that later.

Loading your musket

So you've passed your own musket check, your unit's safety inspection and you are on the march for battle! This is where the proverbial rubber meets the road in reenacting; loading and firing as a battalion, company and in independent fire. However, to do this quickly and safely, there are a few guidelines that you must remember in all of the confusion, noise and heat of battle.

You've reached the battlefield and the command is "By company, into line!" You undouble and hustle into place. Then comes the crucial command. "Load!"

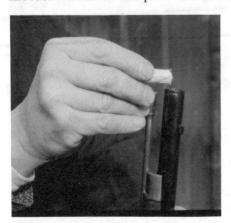

Keep your hands and face clear of your musket muzzle while loading in case of a flashoff!

Remember some *but not all* of the lessons from 'loading in nine times'. You pull a paper cartridge from your cartridge box and tear it with your teeth. Make sure that your musket butt is between your feet with the barrel away from you and the ramrod toward you. Push the muzzle *away from your face* and keep your hands clear of the muzzle as you pour the charge down the bore. Remember that spent cap that you left on the nipple? That is what keeps air from coming in through the nipple opening and mixing with the powder you are pouring down your musket barrel. After a few rounds, your musket will be hot and that air combined with sparks, could ignite your powder charge while you are pouring, burning you severely. *Always leave the spent cap on your musket nipple while loading!* Once your powder is poured, throw the cartridge paper away. *Do not stuff it down the bore* as it will only become a fire hazard in dry weather and pieces may blow back to burn you or your pards.

The Civil War Reenactor's Blackpowder Guide

Under no circumstances should you draw your ramrod, even to "simulate" ramming your charge. **The only time ramrods are used in reenacting is in non-firing demonstrations or in safety inspections.**

So you're loaded, but not capped. The enemy is closing fast and you're in a hurry! You fish the cap out of your pouch and fumble with it as you stuff it over the "cone." You bring up your piece and are ready to blast the enemy, but wait a second! Are you in the rear rank? Before you even *think* about firing, either on command or in independent fire, make sure that when your musket is over your first rank pard's right shoulder and that your filemate's shoulder is aligned between the rear and middle barrel bands of your musket. If you are too far back, you risk getting your musket muzzle too close to your first rank pard's ear. Too close, and now the percussion cap is too near the ear! A little precision goes a long way! **When in any doubt whatever about whether or not to fire, don't!**

So your alignment is good - the enemy is closing. "Ready! Aim!" screams your commander. But how close are they? Are they too close? Use the "rule of thumb". Stick your left thumb up from alongside your musket barrel and see if it will block out an advancing enemy soldier. If an advancing "enemy" soldier appears larger than your thumb, then they are close enough so that you must elevate your muskets so as not to envelop them in hot powder residue. When in doubt, elevate your musket and remind your pards to do the same. *The command "Elevate!" is to be instantly obeyed no matter who issues it!*

But what if you pull the trigger and nothing happens?

Even if you have properly loaded and primed your musket, there's still the possibility that it may not go off when you pull the trigger. If this happens, don't panic. Deduce the cause by process of elimination.

Did the cap explode, or did the hammer fall not exploding the cap? A fired cap usually has the "wings" splayed out from the impact of the hammer and explosion of the cap. If the cap is spent, replace it. Maybe you forgot to prime in the confusion of battle. If the cap has not fired, simply recock the musket (be sure to go to full cock) and try again, either waiting for the command if you are in organized volleying or firing on your own if you are in independent fire.

An expended musket cap has the wings splayed out

The Civil War Reenactor's Blackpowder Guide

If the cap does not explode this time, just try another one. If this replacement cap does explode and the main charge does not fire, then there is a blockage of some kind or the powder charge is wet or contaminated. *Under no circumstances should you pour another charge down the barrel of your musket at this point.* Continue the process of elimination.

Sometimes a powder charge will not pour all the way down the bore but will spread itself out and stick to the bore due to moisture, oil in the barrel or even static electricity. Hold the muzzle of your musket up and rap the breech area of the musket with the flat of your hand. This will sometimes shake loose some of the powder granules stuck to the bore, allowing them to descend into the breech area. Many times, this is all it will take to get the charge to ignite. Try it again.

If you are still unsuccessful, you will have to take a "hit", or turn your musket over to your unit ordnance sergeant or other file closer who will then take your musket at least 30 yards behind the battle line and try to clear it for you. If your file closer cannot clear your musket, *be sure that you dump the powder charge after the battle* and deal with the problem back in camp or at home. **Under no circumstances should you draw a ramrod yourself or otherwise try to clear the musket on the field!** Once back in camp, run as many patches down the bore as needed until they come up dry and clean. If your bore is clean, then there is something else restricting the flash from the cap. Keep in mind that your musket should work perfectly well with the original nipple *if it has been properly maintained.* It is, however, a common practice in many reenactment units to drill out the hole on the threaded end of the nipple to provide a wider path for the flash to follow to reach the main charge. *Drilling is <u>not recommended</u> and should only be undertaken if absolutely necessary after all else fails and only to the minimum diameter needed for consistent firing.* Experience has shown that a 5/64" drill bit will provide a larger flash channel while minimizing the danger of flashbacks through the nipple. It is not recommended that you drill your nipple to any larger diameter than this, however, as flashbacks have been experienced in blank firing with larger diameter flash holes. *Remember also, that if you ever intend to shoot your musket "live", you must change back to a standard nipple before firing. Otherwise, you will risk a flashback through your enlarged nipple opening and possible injury!* Another option is to install a "hot flash" type nipple of the appropriate diameter and thread.

Be very careful not to drill your nipple too much and only do it if absolutely necessary!

If drilling out the nipple does not work, then there is a blockage of some sort in the bolster. In the case of the 1861 Springfield, you should be able to remove the cleanout

The Civil War Reenactor's Blackpowder Guide

screw and use a nipple pick. Sometimes a shot of compressed air will blow out any blockage. If there is still a blockage at this point, don't try to go any further yourself. Take the musket to a competent gunsmith.

Just after the battle, mother.

The enemy may no longer be in view, but your dirty musket certainly is and should command your immediate attention. Remember that black powder residue is highly corrosive and that it doesn't take long for rust to set in, particularly on a hot, humid day.

You should never simply toss your musket into your tent and forget it until the next day's battle. You'd simply be asking for maintenance problems and misfires especially if you fired 40+ rounds today. But the cold refreshments are waiting, it's a blistering hot afternoon and the party is starting so what's one to do? Not to worry! Hydrogen peroxide to the rescue! But remember that it is not a substitute for a thorough cleaning.

For a quick between battles "fix", first, after placing a cleaning patch on the nipple, simply pour hot water down the barrel to fill it about 2/3 full (Remember that Civil War soldiers used to fill musket barrels with whiskey to smuggle popskull into camp!) to soften the fouling, place your tompion (this is its only reenactment function!) in the muzzle. Give the musket a few shakes and remove the tompion and pour the water out, (that God awful black stuff came out of *my* musket?). Give the barrel a chance to cool, unscrew your musket nipple, put your thumb over the nipple hole and pour your barrel a third full of hydrogen peroxide. Then put your other thumb over the end of the barrel and slosh the stuff around for a minute or so. Then unthumb the barrel and pour it out. Repeat two or three times. While doing this, soak the musket nipple in a bottle cap of peroxide. When done, run a couple of patches down the bore to clean it up, dry the nipple, spray the nipple threads with a rust retardant and screw it back in. Then give the bore a quick shot of rust retardant. Remember that this is only an interim measure. There is still a lot of black powder crud in that rifle that you must get out of there, sooner or later.

If you're not into quick fixes and don't mind having black powder residue fall into your tin cup of water or soda (it actually adds an authentic taste!) while you're cleaning your musket, then you can proceed with a full scale scrub using either black powder cleaner or hot, soapy water, whichever you prefer. Hot water poured down the bore usually serves to loosen most of the residue. An old army procedure was to continue with the hot water treatment described above several times until the water comes out clean. Or if you choose, use a plastic bore brush and keep scrubbing and rinsing the brush until it comes out fairly clean. After that, start to run patches down the bore and continue until they come out dry and clean. The nipple, of course, should be removed, and cleaned inside with pipe cleaners and outside with patches or a rag. The inside of the flash hole or bolster should be thoroughly cleaned with cotton swabs soaked in hot, soapy water or

The Civil War Reenactor's Blackpowder Guide

black powder cleaner. You can get into the flash channel inside the bolster with pipe cleaners. Once you are done, run patches soaked in rust retardant or oil as you prefer down the bore and apply a shot of the same in the bolster & nipple. It'll only take you fifteen minutes or so and save you a lot of scrubbing later on when you get home. Remember, a clean musket is a happy musket!

Home again, home again, to prepare to do it all over again!

If you have done a good job of cleaning your musket Saturday, you will only have Sunday's residue to scrub off. However, if you got lazy, some of the stuff is going to be baked on and you will spend an inordinate amount of time scrubbing your bore until you get the crud out. Whatever way you choose, once the musket bore, bolster and nipple are clean, you're still not done!

Two large screws secure the lock mechanism. Barrel tang screw is visible just behind the hammer.

Enfield replica lock mechanism removed for cleaning.

Remove the lock first. In order to do this properly, bring the hammer to the half-cock position. Then back your lock screws out most of the way. Hold your musket so that your thumbs are resting on the lock screw heads. Press on the screws to push the lock out - *never try to pry it loose!* After removing the lock, take your barrel bands off, remove the barrel tang screw. The barrel will then come right out of the stock in your hand. If you have not done this before, you may find a heavy accumulation of black powder residue and/or rust. Needless to say, this must be cleaned off the barrel and stock. Once you are finished, apply rust retardant or engine oil and then begin to reassemble the rifle. When reinstalling the lock mechanism, be sure *not to over tighten the screws!* Check the face of the lock plate in relation to the stock and be sure that the lock screws are not protruding from the lock plate as this is a sure sign of over tightening of the lock screws. Remember that one of the most common reasons that a musket will not hold at half-cock is that the lock has been screwed in too tightly.

You are now ready to either store your musket or hang it over the fireplace as you choose. If you go more than two weeks between events, be sure to take it down and run a

The Civil War Reenactor's Blackpowder Guide

patch through the bore. You'll be surprised at what comes out! Black powder residue seems to sneak out at night and implant itself in your musket regardless of how well you cleaned it! The answer is regular maintenance. When your filemate has incessant misfires at the next event and you don't, the value of meticulous care will self-evident!

Chapter 1 Notes

(1) The button end of the ramrod should be inserted down the bore initially to detect any buildup of fouling and/or unburned powder in the barrel. The gunpowder portion of this residue is usually due to misfires and unless cleaned from the bore immediately after shooting can cause a dangerous explosion of the unburned powder in the barrel which could result in damage to the firearm and injury to the shooter. **(This information thanks to John G. Zimmerman, Master Gunsmith of Harpers Ferry, WV)**

The Civil War Reenactor's Blackpowder Guide

Chapter 3   School of the Carbine

While there are several excellent quality Civil War era replica carbines available, the one that is most widely used in reenacting today is the Sharps pattern carbine and we will therefore use this model as the basis for our discussion. The procedures discussed here are also applicable to the Sharps infantry rifle used by many reenactors portraying Hiram Berdan's Sharpshooters.

Prior to loading

Many of the basic fundamentals are the same as those outlined in the preceding chapter on muskets. The relevant points will be reiterated with focus on use of the breech loading carbine as opposed to the muzzle loading musket.

When you pick up the carbine, be sure to clear it by ensuring that there is neither a live cap on the nipple nor a charge in the bore. After checking the nipple, lower the triggerguard to open the breech and then check the carbine bore for obstructions. This is a bit easier than with the muzzle loading musket, as the Sharps has a falling block type breech action, and with the breech open, it is easy to inspect the bore. Obviously, any leftover hay, horse manure or whatever from previous events can be easily and quickly removed from the bore.

While a Sharps carbine does not have a breech plug, it does have a removable breech block that serves the same purpose and therefore the arm should be checked to ensure that the breech block is clear before firing. After insuring that the bore is clear, cap the carbine and warn bystanders that you are going to fire. Point the carbine in a safe direction, place the muzzle near a leaf or similar object and fire. If the leaf

Sharps replica carbine breechblock lever secured by retaining pin.

The Civil War Reenactor's Blackpowder Guide

Breech block lever rotated forward. Note recessed area that fits into the slot on the breech.

does not move, then there is something obstructing the flash channel.

If there appears to be an obstruction, remove the breech block from the carbine by depressing the spring loaded pin next to the retaining pin lever, turn the lever clockwise and then twist it back and forth while pulling it until the pin comes free of the receiver. The breech block can then be easily removed from the carbine.

Remove the nipple and check it for obstructions. If it is clear, then take out the flash channel screw (which is on the left side of the breech block) and try to remove whatever obstruction there is with cotton swabs and pipe cleaners as illustrated on the next page.

If the mess is too stubborn, which may occur with baked on, years old residue and/or rust, you may have to take a "hit" for the weekend unless you choose to fight with revolvers and saber or can borrow a carbine. If that is the case, wait until you

Breechblock lever and pin partly removed.

get home to deal with your carbine. At that time, put the breech block in a vise and use an electric drill with a bit smaller than the flash channel diameter. With the drill on low speed, try to gently break up the obstruction. If the flash channel has become rusted, you can try to polish the channel out with a Dremel Mototool. If that won't work, you may have to replace the breech block.

If your bore and breech block are clean, the next step is to inspect the nipple, primarily to insure that it is in good repair, not drilled out excessively and is properly

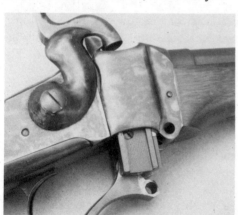

Removing the breech block.

threaded into the breech block. If the nipple does not bottom out in the breech block or if the threads seem exceptionally tight part way in, *do not fire the carbine until you are sure that the nipple is properly seated.* There is the possibility of the nipple blowing out of the

The Civil War Reenactor's Blackpowder Guide

Removing flash channel screw from Sharps breechblock

breech block on firing, which could create a serious and potentially deadly safety hazard as previously described in the chapter on muskets.

As with the diagnosis for the musket, if the nipple seems to be too loose or too tight, check (see Appendix 1) for proper threads for Civil War replica carbines. A thread gauge will tell you if the nipple is correct. If it is not, replace it with the correct one. Again, if the problem persists, *do not attempt to fire the carbine! It should be taken to a competent gunsmith for repair.*

Once you are sure that the nipple is correctly seated and is clear of obstructions, point the carbine in a safe direction and test-fire with a cap holding the muzzle of the carbine in front of a leaf or blade of grass. If the explosion of the cap moves the leaf, you are clear and ready to load. As with the musket, be sure to leave the spent cap on the nipple.

Loading your carbine

Cleaning Sharps breech block flash channel with pipe cleaner.

While loading for the Sharps carbine is

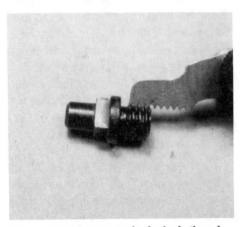

Using a thread gauge to check nipple threads.

quite different than for the musket, proper procedures must still be followed with an eye toward common sense and safety.

Lower the trigger guard to open the breech. Insert a paper cartridge *almost* all the way into the chamber, leaving just a bit protruding from the breech. Some reenactors prefer to make their "Sharps" cartridges slightly under bore size (using a 1/2" dowel for a .54 caliber piece) and roll them quite tight to facilitate quick reloading. After inserting the cartridge, raise the trigger guard which will close the breech, chop off the end of the paper cartridge, and expose the flash channel in the breech to the black powder. *The reason the spent cap is left on the nipple is to keep air from mixing with the powder, which could cause a cookoff or*

The Civil War Reenactor's Blackpowder Guide

Inserting paper cartridge with a 'tail' into the Sharps carbine.

unintentional discharge in a hot gun caused by embers remaining in the breech area when loading.

It is a wise idea after raising the breech to tilt the carbine quickly to the right to dump any excess powder that was left on top of the breech block as the end of the cartridge was chopped off, thereby avoiding the possibility of having it flash off in your face then you fire.

Once loaded, remove the spent cap, recap the carbine and prepare to fire. Before you do, make sure that your pards on either side of you are in a straight line and not ahead of you. The same principle is used here in keeping carbine muzzles as far away from eardrums as possible. Is the "enemy" closing fast? Remember to use the rule of "thumb" to determine proper elevation of your carbine muzzles before firing.

Oh, my God, they're all over me and my carbine won't shoot!

First thing to do is cock it and try again! If your carbine again fails to fire, recap and try again. If it still won't shoot and there are too many fellows in the wrong color coats coming your way, use your revolver!

Sharps breechblock about to slice end from 'tail' of paper cartridge

Sharps carbine loaded, capped and ready to go.

Once you have driven off the bluebellies or graybacks as the case may be (or fallen valiantly in the attempt!), you can then return your attention to your carbine back in camp in a more relaxed environment. *Under no circumstances should you try to clear the carbine on the field beyond the aforementioned immediate action.*

The Civil War Reenactor's Blackpowder Guide

Back in camp, you may investigate the cause of the problem by using the process of elimination similar to the methodology used for the musket. If the cap has not exploded, replace it and try again. If the cap goes off, but the main charge does not, then there is a blockage of some sort, or the powder charge is wet and/or contaminated. This is an easier problem to deal with in the case of a carbine than a musket. Simply open the breech (be careful as there will be loose powder from the unfired load) and rap the breech end of your carbine with the flat of your hand while holding it butt end down.

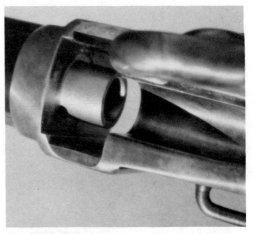

Removable combustion chamber liner partly removed from Sharps carbine.

This should dislodge the paper cartridge and any loose powder. If you can't clear the bore at this point, use your cleaning kit to clear the bore and then wipe it dry.

Carbine cleaning, simple and easy

Once the fight is over, cleaning the Sharps is a snap. Simply lower the breech block and scrub the black powder residue out of the bore until patches come through clean. Be sure to leave the breech block in place until after cleaning the bore as it holds your firing chamber liner in place and it could be easily lost. Either black powder cleaner or hot or soapy water can be used for

Forward face of breechblock where flash channel enters the breech.

this task as you prefer.

Once the bore is clean, only then remove the breech block as previously described in this chapter. If your carbine has a removable firing chamber liner be sure to slide it out to clean both it and the chamber well as it will trap quite a bit of black powder residue.

Sharps carbine brechblock well with breech block removed.

The Civil War Reenactor's Blackpowder Guide

Then, unscrew and clean the nipple. Next, remove the flash channel screw on the left side of the breech block and use pipe cleaners to clean the flash channel. Use cotton swabs and pipe cleaners to clean the recessed area where the flash channel enters the breech.

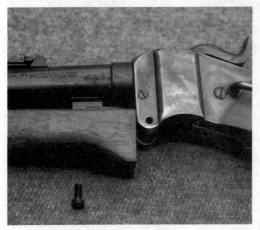
Sharps carbine fore-end removed.

Once the breech block is clean inside and outside, replace the flash channel screw and nipple. Laying the breech block aside, clean the breech block well in the receiver of the carbine. Then lubricate the mating surfaces of the chamber liner (if so equipped) and the breech block and replace these parts in the carbine. You are now ready for the next day's fight.

Maintenance at home

As with the musket, it is prudent to periodically remove the carbine forearm and clean out the black powder residue that always seems to find its way in there. Sometimes black powder granules can accumulate there if care is not taken to hold muzzle up when closing the breech and chopping off the end of the paper cartridge. Similarly, you will find all kinds of black powder residue in the lockwork of your carbine,

Two screws in left side of receiver and saddle bar secure lockwork in the Sharps carbine.

so it to should be removed and cleaned once or twice a year. This is easily accomplished by removing the two screws that secure the lockwork to the stock. The lock plate can then be easily removed for cleaning. Remember never to pry the lock mechanism out - push on the lock screws after loosening them to remove it. When replacing the lock, also remember to be careful not to overtighten the lock screws.

Lockwork removed from Sharps carbine for cleaning.

The Civil War Reenactor's Blackpowder Guide

Chapter 4   School of the Revolver

There are a wide variety of Civil War era replica revolvers available today. Some are extremely authentic replicas and others less so, but most still function reliably and safely. The vast majority of replica revolvers used in Civil War reenacting are either Colt style Model 1851 Navy or Model 1860 Army or are of the Remington Model of 1858 pattern. As these are the most common replicas found in the Civil War reenacting hobby, we will use the Colt and Remington pattern revolvers as the basis for our discussion.

Should I be carrying a revolver at all?

The most fundamental question is whether you should carry a revolver at all as a reenactor. If you portray an infantryman, most event sponsors will not allow you to carry one and limit revolvers to officers and some NCO's simply as a safety measure. Usually all cavalrymen, regardless of rank, and some artillery NCO's and officers are armed with revolvers.

Reenactors who intend to carry revolvers must make their own decisions regarding the type to purchase. This decision should be based on a variety of factors - whether you are a Federal or a Confederate, what unit you belong to, and other practical and historic factors. Obviously, a lieutenant in a Union infantry unit would not normally be found to be carrying an exotic piece such as the LeMat, which was supplied to the Confederacy exclusively. Neither would a Federal or Confederate officer in an early war impression be carrying such a model as the Rogers and Spencer, which was not manufactured until 1865 and was never officially issued.

If you do decide to purchase a revolver or revolvers, use common sense and practicality in making your choice. Many cavalry reenactors prefer the Remington pattern simply because of its easy cylinder interchangability, thereby allowing greater firepower potential. Others prefer the esthetic lines of the Colt series. Try to combine whatever appeals to you with authenticity and practicality when choosing your armament.

The Civil War Reenactor's Blackpowder Guide

Replica M1851 Navy cylinder. Note safety pins between nipples.

There is an important safety issue in regard to the Colt style replica revolvers. Some manufacturers of higher quality Colt replicas manufacture their revolver cylinders with safety pins between each chamber just as Sam Colt did during the 1850's and 1860's. These pins are used to keep the hammer in place between chambers when the revolver is loaded to prevent an accidental discharge. If at all possible, you should purchase a replica equipped with cylinder safety pins. If your revolver is not equipped with safety pins, *then you should only load five chambers, leaving the hammer down on an empty chamber.* If you leave the hammer down on a live and capped chamber or set it between live chambers without a safety pin to secure it when you carry it in a holster, you run the risk of an accidental discharge which could cause severe injury and/or property damage.

The hammer is held in place by the safety pin and cannot slip off thereby causing a dangerous accidental discharge.

Steel or brass revolver frames?

There are on the market a variety of brass framed replica revolvers, of both the Colt and Remington pattern. A few words are in order here regarding authenticity and durability of these pieces.

Typical Colt 1851 Navy replica revolver, 2d model with squareback triggerguard

According to several reliable historical publications **(1)**, Sam Colt did not make any of his percussion revolvers with brass frames, nor was the Remington revolver manufactured using brass frames. Only steel was used for the frames in the originals of both Colt and Remington revolvers, although brass was used for trigger guards of both the Colt M1860 and the Remington M1858 and was used for both trigger guard and

The Civil War Reenactor's Blackpowder Guide

Remington M1858 Army revolver replica

backstrap of some Colt M1851 Navy Models.

However, several Confederate revolvers were manufactured with brass frames, most notably the Griswold and Gunnison **(2)**, which was based on the Colt M1851 Navy and the Spiller and Burr **(3)**, which bore a slight resemblance to the M1858 Remington in that it had a solid frame with a top strap. Replicas of these two pieces, in addition to the current Colt and Remington brass framed replicas, as well as several "generic" brass framed pieces are available on the replica percussion revolver market today. Interestingly, while both steel and brass framed 1851 Navy and similarly styled replicas are currently offered in both .36 and .44 caliber, all of the originals, both Colt and period copies, were only made in .36 caliber. **(4)**

The reenactor should make an educated decision about whether to purchase a steel or brass framed revolver based on its planned use. You should also remember, that brass, being a softer metal than steel, is going to be affected by continued hard use. The most common complaint about brass framed revolvers is that they eventually go out of "time", meaning that each chamber of the cylinder will no longer exactly line up with the barrel when the revolver is placed in the full cock position. This happens because of slight changes in the interior specifications of the brass frame which is eventually affected by heat and impact of constant recoil of the revolver. While this most often happens when a brass framed revolver is fired live continually with heavy loads, it is not unknown in reenactor revolvers. The only remedy is to have a competent gunsmith retime the revolver.

Prior to loading

Be sure to clear the revolver as soon as you pick it up. Place it in the half-cock position, point the muzzle straight up and rotate the cylinder, checking each nipple and chamber to be sure none are charged. After clearing, then check to be sure that your revolver bore and each of the cylinder chambers are clear of any obstruction. An easy way to do this is to run a wooden dowel or cleaning rod of the appropriate diameter down the bore. Be sure that the rod is at least three inches longer than the barrel (8" for Colt 1860's and 1858 Remingtons; 7 1/2" for Colt 1851 Navies) so that it will reach to the bottom of the cylinder chambers. Once you are sure that the bore and cylinder chambers are clear, you should "cap off" the revolver in similar fashion to the musket, to clear any oil in the nipples and make sure that there are no blockages. Cap all six nipples, let your pards know that you are test firing, be sure that your revolver is pointed in a safe direction and discharge all six chambers at a leaf or blade of grass. If the explosions of each cap disturb the leaf, the nipples are clear. If not, the offending nipples should be removed and cleaned or replaced. Once you are sure the revolver is clear, you are ready to load.

The Civil War Reenactor's Blackpowder Guide

There has been, and still continues to be, much discussion in the Civil War reenactment community about proper procedures and proper materials for loading of revolvers. After all, unlike a musket or carbine, the powder charges must be "secured" in each chamber to prevent losing them when the revolver is turned muzzle down and holstered after loading. The materials that have been used to secure blank charges in the past range from peanut butter and wrapping paper to "Wonder Wads".

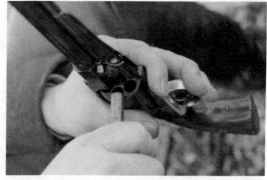

Loading "cold" revolver from a flask while rotating the cylinder with the left index finger.

Loading the revolver from a paper cartridge.

Suffice it to say that <u>any material that could become a projectile or create a fire hazard</u> absolutely cannot be loaded in a revolver used for reenacting! This immediately rules out Wonder Wads or <u>any kind of paper wadding</u>. The sole exception to this rule is the use of nitrated paper cartridges which combust with the black powder and leave no burning residue.

The most commonly used and most practical material to secure revolver loads in the chambers is cream of wheat and we will therefore use it exclusively in our discussion. When compressed, it will secure the loads in your revolver chambers, even when the revolver is carried on horseback or otherwise bounced around. It is also very easy to use. But we'll get to that later as we cover the loading procedure step-by-step. For those of you who still wish to use peanut butter (it really does work), Bon Appetit!

Loading your revolver

Place your revolver in the half-cock position, hold it muzzle up in one hand so that you can readily turn the cylinder with your index finger. You can load powder from a flask only if the revolver is "cold" or unfired. However, if you intend to load in the field after firing, you must use paper cartridges as any spark from a hot revolver could cause the flask to explode like a hand grenade. Many reenactors prefer to use paper cartridges exclusively simply for this reason.

The Civil War Reenactor's Blackpowder Guide

Compressing revolver charges with loading lever.

Whether using cartridge or flask, fill each chamber of the revolver with the powder charges recommended by the manufacturer. These charges are usually 25 - 30 grains for the Colt 1860 Army and Remington 1858 Army in .44 caliber and 15 -20 grains for the Colt 1851 Navy in .36 caliber. If you make paper cartridges, load them accordingly with the proper powder charge for your revolver. Be sure to *hold the revolver so that it is pointed away from you as you load in case of premature discharge.*

Once you have loaded the chambers of your revolver with the prescribed amount of black powder, you are then ready to insert cream of wheat into each chamber to secure your powder charges (provided you haven't eaten it all for breakfast!). The easiest flask for this purpose is the round type with the ends that unscrew, which makes refilling the flask an easy job. Pour the cream of wheat from the flask spout until each chamber is full. Employ your loading lever to compress the cream of wheat to hold the charges in each chamber. You are now ready to cap your revolver.

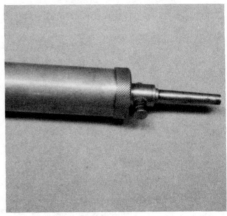

A round flask with ends that screw on is a practical choice for cream of wheat.

Most .36 and .44 caliber Colt and Remington replica revolvers have nipples that are a bit small for the standard #11 percussion cap. Even the #10 cap will sometimes be a little bit loose. When capping your revolver, it is best to give each cap a little squeeze to make sure that it stays put on the nipple. Then just slide it on, guiding with your fingers and seating it with your thumb.

Seating percussion cap on the revolver nipple.

Now you are ready to fire!

If you are an infantry officer, you will usually have no need to fire your revolver unless your troops are in danger of being overrun. If that occurs, always move to the flank of your company or battalion to make sure that you have a clear field of fire. Once you have done so, move forward and stay several feet "down line" from your troops to make sure

The Civil War Reenactor's Blackpowder Guide

that your revolver will be well away from any of your infantrymen before you fire. If you are within a couple of feet of your infantrymen, then a good rule is to extend your revolver forward so that the muzzle is beyond the second band of your infantry soldiers' musket. This way, you will also have a "buffer zone", with your ears midway between your soldier's percussion caps and musket muzzles. Be sure also to never fire a revolver from the rear rank.

So they're closing fast and you are ready to "repel the invaders." *Remember the rule of thumb!* Just because the revolver was designed as a close quarters arm *does not necessarily mean that you should use it as such in reenacting.* You should elevate your revolver just as a musket should be elevated at the same appropriate ranges. If quarters get really close, such as inside 25 feet, *you should not fire at all unless you have room to elevate and turn at least 30 degrees away from your intended "target".* When in doubt, <u>do not fire!</u>

Loading the revolver in the field

You mean these six lovely shots are all I get and then my battle's over? Unless you have a Remington M1858 and spare cylinders handy (be sure to carry the spare cylinders loaded, but not capped as a jolt or jar could set off one or more chambers), then I guess that your battle is over. However, if you are ready to reload during a lull in the fight (which is exactly what our Civil War ancestors did!), then you can carry on the battle!

In order to do this, you may have to learn some different ways of holding your revolver to load. Who knows where you will be? You may not be able to sit and hold the pistol to load. You may have to do it while standing. Or lying down! A necessary skill to master then, is that of holding the revolver in one hand and rotating the cylinder with your fingers, as you pour powder and cream of wheat successively into each of the revolver chambers. Then ram with the loading lever as before and recap your revolver to complete your loading procedure. A practiced Civil War reenactment pistoleer who is properly prepared with cartridges and cream of wheat should be able to reload in the field in fairly short order.

One very important note - if you do not fire all of the rounds from your revolver during an engagement and then reload in the field, be sure to *remove the live percussion caps from the unfired chambers before proceeding to reload the ones you have fired!* No percussion revolver should ever be loaded with live caps on the nipples. Once reloaded, you may then recap all of the revolver's nipples and you are ready to go!

An easy way of carrying revolver ammunition is to simply load the prescribed amount of powder into the paper tubes that you make up for your musket, but then cut off the excess paper as the powder charge is smaller. Then fold over and glue as you normally would. These "miniature" cartridges will fit very neatly into a pistol cartridge box. You can carry quite a few with you by loading the box in two "tiers" with a piece of

The Civil War Reenactor's Blackpowder Guide

cardboard cut to fit to separate to tiers of cartridges. Your cream of wheat flask can go in your haversack.

But what if my revolver doesn't fire?

You have an edge on your musket toting pards on this one! Just cock the revolver and fire again! However, once you have fired all of the rounds in your cylinder, you should then identify the misfired chamber, place the revolver on half-cock, and rotate the chamber to the next firing position. Cock and pull the trigger. If the chamber again fails to fire, remove the cap, exploded or not, and place a fresh cap on the offending nipple. If this fresh cap explodes, but the powder in the chamber underneath does not, then there is obviously some sort of blockage restricting the flash from the percussion cap or the powder is possibly wet and/or contaminated. If this is the case, *don't try to do anything else in the field. The offending chamber must be cleared back in camp.*

Cleaning your revolver

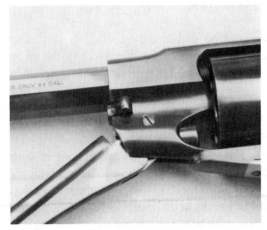

Note hand hold on tip of M1858 Remington cylinder pin

Your revolver is a more complex firearm than either a musket or a carbine. Due to its more complicated nature, the required measure of maintenance is a bit more involved. We will cover the "lick and a promise" maintenance that is really reserved for the Saturday afternoon cleaning "between battles" and the more involved and thorough cleaning you must give your revolver if you want it to give you years of reliable service.

If you have only fired six to twelve rounds from your revolver in the course of the day's fight, you can probably get away with an abbreviated cleaning to tide you over to the next day's battle. If you have fired more, then you probably have generated enough black powder fouling to warrant a thorough disassembly and cleaning which will be covered in detail in a subsequent paragraph.

Quick Cleaning

For this procedure, you can use either hot or soapy water or black powder cleaner depending upon your personal preference. Use a pistol cleaning rod of the correct length and screw in a plastic bristle brush of the

Removing Remington M1858 cylinder. Note left index finger holding loading lever.

29

The Civil War Reenactor's Blackpowder Guide

appropriate caliber. Dip the brush in cleaning solvent or water and run it all the way down the bore into the revolver chamber. Give it a quick twist to loosen any crud in the chamber. Pull back out and rinse in clean water. Cock the revolver, advancing to the next chamber and let the hammer down gently. Repeat the process for all six chambers. The repeated scrubbing will get most of the fouling out of the bore.

Loosening M1851 Navy Colt barrel wedge screw.

Remove the cleaning rod bristle tip and replace with a slotted tip. Repeat the process, using a clean patch for each cylinder chamber. However, fold the patch over the tip of the rod so as to clean the bottom of each chamber. After all six cylinder chambers are clean, run another clean patch down to make sure most of the fouling is out. Once you are sure the bore and chambers are reasonably clean, run a patch soaked in a commercial rust retardant down into each chamber.

Engage between chambers

Lift barrel from cylinder pin.

After you have completed the bore and chamber cleaning exercise, place the revolver on half-cock, and then clean the inside of each nipple with a pipe cleaner soaked in rust retardant and the outside of the nipples with cotton swabs, similarly moistened. This ten minute process will assure you of a relatively clean revolver for the next day's battle, but nothing more. If for some reason you do not use your revolver the next day, be sure to properly clean it after you arrive home.

After the Sunday battle, you can either give your revolver a thorough cleaning on the spot, or give it a thorough blast with rust retardant and complete your maintenance after you get home.

A more thorough revolver cleaning is really necessary between events.

I have seen more than one fine replica blackpowder revolver rendered totally useless due to improper or inadequate maintenance. These sins ranged from seized nipples to rusted out bores and cylinders. Make no mistake about the fact that if you do not properly maintain your revolver, it will not function. Our Civil War ancestors clearly understood this as their lives were on the line. While their maintenance procedures then

The Civil War Reenactor's Blackpowder Guide

were a bit crude by our standards today, their revolvers did perform well for them in battle. Take care of yours and it will too!

There is a bit more work involved with a revolver than there is for a musket or carbine and you must disassemble it to clean it thoroughly. Not to worry! It's easy than you think. Read on! Removal of the cylinder is mandatory as the nipples must come out and the cylinder and the pin on which it rotates must be cleaned.

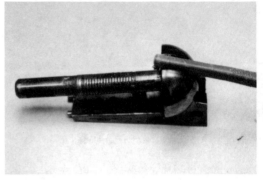

For the Remington models, this is a relatively simple procedure involving dropping the loading lever just far enough to expose the tip on the end of the cylinder pin. Grasp the pin and pull out. (A new revolver may require a tap on the end of the cylinder pin with a plastic hammer to loosen it.) With the cylinder pin in the withdrawn position (it is held in the revolver frame by the loading lever pivot screw, so don't try to pull it free), pull back on the hammer slightly and the cylinder should come right out in your hand. Use the index finger of the left hand to hold the loading lever from coming all the way down.

Be sure to clean black powder residue from the hammer channel. Modern M-16 rifle "toothbrush" works well for this and other close quarters tasks.

Two upper backstrap screws - M1851 Colt Navy

Colt pattern revolvers all come apart in a different way. First, loosen the barrel wedge screw. You needn't take it all the way out if you choose not to. Then, place the revolver on its left side atop a couple of wood blocks or similar support so that the wedge will have room to come out unimpeded. Using a brass punch, gently tap the wedge from the right until it drops out. (You should have an old towel spread on your workbench for this type of cleaning operation.) Once the wedge is out, place the revolver in the half-cock position, which will position the cylinder so that the loading lever will engage between chambers. Use the loading lever to move the barrel out from the cylinder and then remove it completely. At this point, the cylinder will slide right off the pin.

An historical (and maintenance) note is in order at this point about Colt revolvers. A perennial complaint about the original Colt revolver inherent in the design was that it would "shoot loose", that is, the backstrap and trigger guard screws would tend to loosen with extended use. Your replica will probably act accordingly over a reenacting season. If

The Civil War Reenactor's Blackpowder Guide

you check all six of these screws at this point in your "field stripping", you will likely find one or more that are loose. Tighten them up before you proceed further.

Three screws secure the Colt pattern triggerguard.

Once the cylinder is out of the gun, the nipples should be removed and cleaned inside with pipe cleaners and outside with cotton swabs and patches or a rag. Remember that the nipples must <u>*always be removed and cleaned or they will rust into place!*</u> The barrel and cylinder chambers may be cleaned with hot or soapy water or blackpowder cleaning solvent as you wish as described in the "field cleaning" paragraph. Once patches come through clean, use rust preventative solution to protect the bore and chambers. Nooks and crannies in the barrel, frame and cylinder are easily cleaned with a combination of cotton swabs and pipe cleaners. Be sure to clean inside the hammer channel making sure to remove any percussion cap fragments you may discover as they will surely cause a jam and a resultant misfire. Other areas that require special attention are the loading lever and rammer which should be removed from the gun and cleaned separately. Once you are satisfied with the cleanliness of all these parts, you can then reassemble the revolver. Some reenactors prefer to leave their revolvers disassembled overnight and then clean all the parts again before reassembly. Not a bad idea!

You're not done yet!

Actually, the above procedure is sufficient between events. However, at least once a year, or more often if you have a heavy event schedule, the lockwork should be removed from your revolver and thoroughly cleaned. This is actually a lot easier than it sounds. The disassembly procedures for the Colt and Remington are a bit different, so I will cover each separately.

Disassembling the Colt lockwork

After removing the barrel assembly and cylinder as described previously, next remove your Colt pattern revolver's three backstrap screws. There are two, that secure the backstrap to the frame, and one at the bottom that secures to the triggerguard. This will allow you to remove the backstrap and the one piece wood grip. The next step is to remove the mainspring screw, and then the mainspring itself. Once this is accomplished, the three

'Colt M1851 Mainspring'

32

The Civil War Reenactor's Blackpowder Guide

screws securing the trigger guard, to which the mainspring is attached, may be removed, allowing the trigger guard to be removed from the revolver frame. All that remains now,

Hammer & hand being removed from 1851 Navy Colt.

is to remove the lockwork itself. Invert the revolver frame and remove the screw securing the cylinder bolt spring. This spring keeps tension on the trigger, allowing it to return after firing and on the cylinder bolt, which stops the cylinder in proper alignment with the barrel. Remove this spring. Then place the revolver frame on its right side. Remove the two small screws in the frame which secure the cylinder bolt and trigger. Be sure to place the screws that secure each part separately from the others after cleaning so that they may be readily identified for reassembly. After removing these two screws, remove the trigger and bolt (note the corrosive powder residue on these parts!). Next, remove the larger hammer screw. Then, gently pull the hammer down in the frame. The hand and its spring, which are attached to the hammer with a pin should come out with it. Your Colt style revolver is now completely stripped to the frame.

Disassembling the Remington lockwork

Interestingly, the Remington, also being a single action revolver, functions very much like the Colt. However, the construction of the revolver and its mechanism is somewhat different. The first major difference is that the Remington is a solid frame revolver; only the trigger guard is removable. The second

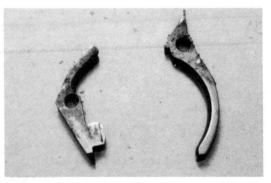

Cylinder bolt (left) and trigger (right) for 1851 Navy Colt. Note black powder residue on these parts!

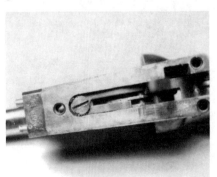

Colt cylinder bolt spring.

difference is that one screw is used in place of the two that the Colt uses to hold the trigger and bolt.

After insuring that the revolver is unloaded and removing the cylinder, then remove the screw that holds the two pieces of the grip onto the frame and remove the grips. This

33

The Civil War Reenactor's Blackpowder Guide

will expose the mainspring. First loosen the screw that secures it to the toe of the butt. This also releases tension on the mainspring. To remove the mainspring, simply slide it out. Next, invert the pistol and remove the triggerguard screw and the triggerguard itself. This will expose the trigger bolt spring and the lockwork. Remove the trigger bolt spring screw and spring. At this point, turn the revolver with its left side up and remove the small screw

Removing Remington M1858 mainspring.

M1858 Remington hammer & hand at bottom of frame.

in the frame. This secures the trigger and the bolt, which will both easily come right out of the gun once the screw securing them has been removed. The hammer screw should then be removed. Next, gently slide the hammer and the hand down and out of the frame as far they will go, thus exposing the screw that holds the hand onto the hammer. Remove this screw and slide the hand down and out of the frame. Once this is done, the hammer may be removed by sliding it up and out of the top of the frame. The last items to be removed are the rammer and loading lever which come out of the gun as one unit once the screw securing them has been removed. Once the loading lever is out, then slide the cylinder pin forward and out of the frame. This completes the disassembly of your Remington pattern revolver.

Your lockwork pieces should then be thoroughly cleaned in your favorite combination of hot, soapy water or blackpowder cleaner and then lightly lubricated, particularly at points where there is metal to metal contact. Congratulations! The cleaning process for your blackpowder revolver is now complete!

Oh My God, how do I put this thing back together?

Not to worry! Actually, your revolver goes back together almost as you took it apart. Be sure to lightly lubricate all bearing surfaces and moving parts where they contact one another. To reassemble the Colt, put the hand pin into the slot in the

1851 Navy Colt wedge spring properly seated.

The Civil War Reenactor's Blackpowder Guide

hammer and slide the hammer/hand assembly gently into the pistol and secure it with the hammer screw. In the case of the Remington, slide the hammer down through the frame from the top and slide the hand and spring up into the frame until the hole in the hand aligns with the threaded hole in the hammer. Then install the screw that secures the hand to the hammer, slide the hammer and hand up into position and replace the hammer screw.

Colt frame pins properly aligned with holes in barrel lug.

The trigger and bolt are then replaced and secured with their screws (one screw in the Remington and two screws in the Colt.) You may need to use needle-nose pliers to correctly position the bolt stop where it contacts the hammer. At this point, the multi-function cylinder bolt spring, which maintains proper pressure to lock the cylinder as it turns as well as returns the trigger to its original position after firing, must be replaced. Be sure that the spring engages the trigger and the cylinder bolt correctly. Then tighten the screw.

The next step in reassembly of both the Remington and Colt is to replace the trigger guard assembly. Remember that only one screw secures the Remington and three secure the Colt.

Replacing hammer & hand in Colt 1851 Navy.

Be sure to lightly lubricate all moving parts such as this hand pin for the Colt pattern revolver.

Then replace the mainspring and the tighten the screw that secures it. This procedure is quite similar for the Remington and the Colt. After replacing the mainspring, the Colt backstrap and grip must then be reassembled to the triggerguard and frame with the appropriate screws as they were dismantled. The Remington grip, which is a two-piece affair, must then be replaced and secured with the screw that hold the pieces to the frame.

The Civil War Reenactor's Blackpowder Guide

The loading lever should then be replaced in the revolver. The procedure is similar for both the Colt and Remington excepting that the cylinder pin must be reinstalled in the Remington prior to assembling the loading lever.

After installing the nipples in the cylinder, the last item to be assembled to the frame is the cylinder. In the case of the Remington, this is a simple procedure of holding the revolver with the hammer just below the half-cock position at which point the

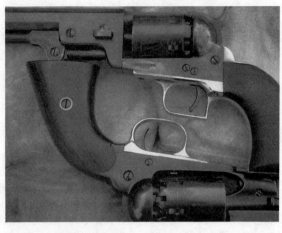

Colt 1851 Navy (top) has three screw lockwork Remington 1858 (bottom) uses only two.

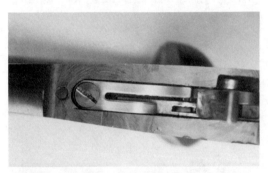

M1858 Remington cylinder bolt spring in place.

cylinder will slide right in place. The cylinder pin should then be moved rearward to secure the cylinder in place.

Installation of the Colt cylinder is a bit different. First, place the revolver on half-cock. Then slide the cylinder onto the cylinder pin. The barrel with its loading lever assembly will then slide onto the cylinder pin. Be sure to align the two pins in the base of the frame with the holes in the barrel. Once the barrel is in place, then slide the wedge into its slot as far as you can by hand. Then engage the wedge pin screw and bring it up a turn or so. With a plastic or brass hammer, gently rap the wedge until the spring tip which keeps it in place has engaged the right side of the barrel lug. Once the wedge is in place, the wedge screw should be secured.

Your revolver is now properly cleaned and ready for next year's campaigns!

The Civil War Reenactor's Blackpowder Guide

Chapter 4 Notes

(1) Frank A. Belden & Charles T. Haven, *A History of the Colt Revolver*, (New York, NY, Bonanza Books), 44, 63, 82, 99; Norm Flayderman, *Guide to Antique American Arms and their values 6th Edition,* (Northbrook, IL, DBI Books, 1994), 71-77, 80-82, 138-140; J.E. Serven, *Colt Firearms from 1836,* (Harrisburg, PA, Stackpole Books, 1981), 55, 71, 74, 118, 131.

(2) Frank A. Belden & Charles T. Haven, *A History of the Colt Revolver*, (New York, NY, Bonanza Books), 122; Norm Flayderman, *Guide to Antique American Arms and their values 6th Edition,* (Northbrook, IL, DBI Books, 1994), 526; J.E. Serven, *Colt Firearms from 1836,* (Harrisburg, PA, Stackpole Books, 1981), 139, 141.

(3) Norm Flayderman, *Guide to Antique American Arms and their values 6th Edition,* (Northbrook, IL, DBI Books, 1994), 529.

(4) Frank A. Belden & Charles T. Haven, *A History of the Colt Revolver*, (New York, NY, Bonanza Books), 67, 70, 74, 75, 77, 78, 122, 123, 124, 125, 126, 128, Norm Flayderman, *Guide to Antique American Arms and their values 6th Edition,* (Northbrook, IL, DBI Books, 1994), 75, 76, 316, 317, 524, 525, 526, 527, 528, 529, J.E. Serven, *Colt Firearms from 1836,* (Harrisburg, PA, Stackpole Books, 1981), 139 - 142.

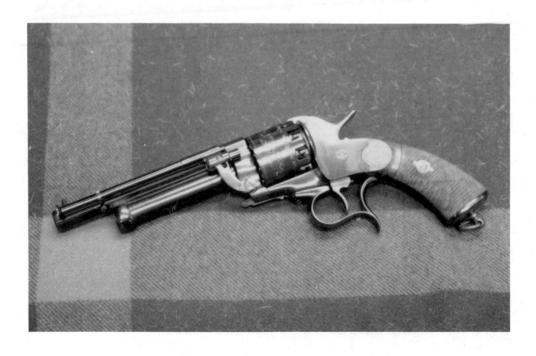

The Civil War Reenactor's Blackpowder Guide

Chapter 5 Specialty Replica Firearms

There are a variety of "specialty" or unusual Civil War era firearms that one may encounter in the reenactment hobby, both original and replica. While some reenactors do use originals and some events continue to allow their use, I continue to feel, as I have commented previously, that use of original firearms is an unwise practice and I will therefore reserve comments for known replicas of original firearms.

Henry rifle replica breech. Plunger at forward end of breech indicates an empty magazine.

Henry Rifle - Although about 14,000 were produced between 1860 and 1865, remember that from an authenticity standpoint, very few Henry's (about 1,700 or so) were actually purchased by the Union Army.**(1)** However, at least one unit did equip itself with Henry rifles at its own expense **(2)** and some were purchased privately by staff officers and others. The replica of this predecessor to the Winchester lever action series may be used in reenactments with plastic molded blank cartridges available from several sources. Be sure that the type you use is designed for the plastic case to split in the front from the force of the explosion as shown in the photograph and that no wads are used in the manufacture of the cartridges as they become

Plastic blank Henry cartridges. The one on the right is expended.

The Civil War Reenactor's Blackpowder Guide

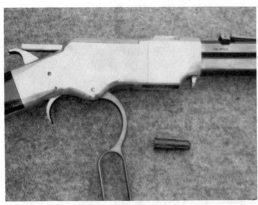

Henry rifle with breech open, lever fully descended which raises the elevator to feed a fresh cartridge from the magazine. Plastic blank cartridge directly below the elevator in the breech of the rifle.

projectiles.

Like any other firearm, the Henry rifle should always be checked to be sure it is clear before being handled. This is accomplished by first pointing the arm in a safe direction (when in doubt, straight up), opening the breech by lowering the lever all the way and checking the firing chamber and elevator to insure that no ammunition is present. The Henry rifle is loaded by sliding the plunger, shown at the breech of the unloaded rifle, out to the muzzle end of the rifle and rotating it, together with the end of the magazine which securing the plunger and its compressed swivels, approximately 45 degrees to the right, spring and opening up the magazine tube, located beneath the barrel and actually an integral part of it, so that cartridges may be loaded. *Remember that the primer of each cartridge in a tubular magazine rests on the nose of that behind it and if violently impacted, could cause the primer and cartridge to detonate inside the magazine! For this reason, care must be taken while loading cartridges into the magazine and particularly when returning the swivel end of the barrel to its original position. The plunger must be held firmly against its spring pressure and then gently be allowed*

Upper portion of Henry magazine tube swiveled to facilitate loading.

to contact the nose of the uppermost cartridge in the magazine.

The Henry is operated by lowering the lever which action extracts and ejects the empty cartridge case, cocks the hammer and activates the elevator, raising a fresh cartridge from the magazine. Returning the lever to its original position pushes the fresh cartridge forward from the elevator, chambering it and making the rifle ready to fire.

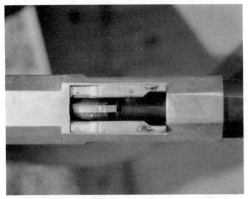

Plastic blank cartridge being pushed by the bolt from the elevator to the firing chamber.

The Civil War Reenactor's Blackpowder Guide

Gently let Henry rifle plunger down to contact nose of the uppermost cartridge.

Remember when cleaning your Henry, that the flash powder used in blank cartridges, like black powder, is as corrosive to brass as it is to steel and that your Henry (unless you have a rare steel frame replica) receiver and elevator are made of brass. Either way, scrub the bore and scrub the receiver inside and out. After wiping the rifle down, it is usually a good idea to leave it in your shop overnight and go over it again the next day, just to be sure.

Maynard Carbine - While not as widely used as other breech loading carbines, the Maynard is a very practical carbine. Unfortunately, there have been very few replicas of the Maynard manufactured to date. The only specimen that the author has seen bears serial # 188 and was made by Harpers Ferry Arms Company, a now defunct replica manufacturer.

The Maynard carbine is the model of simplicity in operation. Lowering the trigger guard tilts the barrel forward, allowing the arm to be cleared

Maynard carbine breech. Note rim of brass cartridge case visible between barrel and breech

by visually inspecting the chamber. Loading is accomplished by insertion of a *metallic cartridge specifically designed for the Maynard* into the breech. This cartridge case has a small hole in the base to allow the flash from the percussion cap to ignite the powder therein. For blank charges, some minor drilling of the hole, not recommended larger than 5/64" may be required for positive ignition. <u>Under no circumstances should cartridge cases drilled for blank shooting be used for live fire as a dangerous flashback through the nipple may result.</u>

Maynard cartridge partly inserted in barrel. Wide cartridge case rim designed for easy grip.

The Civil War Reenactor's Blackpowder Guide

Blank cartridges for the Maynard may be loaded simply by pouring a measured charge of 30 to 35 grains into the cartridge case and compressing slightly (a 1/2" dowel with a .45 ACP cartridge case pushed onto the end as a tamper works very well for this). Once the powder is slightly compressed, then fill it the rest of the

Wide rimmed Maynard cartridge case. Note flash hole in center.

Maynard cartridge case filled with black powder & cream of wheat. Tamping rod tipped with .45 ACP case.

way with cream of wheat and then compress as much as possible. This can be done simply by applying downward pressure by leaning on the dowel or by cutting the dowel down and inserting the cartridge case into a modern reloading press (only where it can be fitted without damaging the thin rim) and using it for compression.

Cleaning procedures for the Maynard are similar to those for any breech loading carbine. Remember that the brass cartridge cases must also be cleaned promptly or they will corrode and deteriorate.

Smith Carbine This carbine, together with the Sharps,

Closeup of Smith carbine breech area.

Spencer and Burnside was one of the most widely used breech loading carbines in the Civil War.**(3)** Replicas are available today from several sources.

Smith carbine cartridge cases, brass (left) and aluminum (right).

As the Smith carbine is a breechloader, inspection and safety procedures are similar to those used for the Sharps pattern carbine. The original Smith carbines were used with either a

The Civil War Reenactor's Blackpowder Guide

rubber or "patent foil" and paper cartridge with a small perforation in the base to allow the percussion cap flash to reach the black powder charge. Reenactors can use either reproduction machined brass or aluminum cartridge cases, both of which can be loaded with black powder and cream of wheat in similar fashion to the Maynard cartridge described in an earlier paragraph. The Smith carbine is a simple "break-top" design, with a hinge in front of the trigger guard. The action is opened by pushing up on the brass lifter in front of the trigger. This lifts the spring catch from the stud on the breech, allowing for opening of the breech up to a 90 degree angle and insertion of a cartridge, after which, the breech is closed and a percussion cap placed on the nipple in similar fashion to the Maynard. Care must be taken *not to reverse the cartridge when loading as it has no rim!*

Loading the Smith carbine.

Spencer rifles and carbines

The Spencer repeating rifle (and later carbine) was a relatively late war innovation, as the first shipment of rifles to the army was made in December of 1862 **(4)** although not in sufficient numbers to have a major effect on the war. However, the carbine version of this revolutionary repeater began to be delivered to the Federal cavalry in October of 1863 with sufficient quantities coming into their hands in 1864 and 1865 to make a major impact in the war effort, being credited by some with shortening the war. **(5)**

Spencer rifle with breech block in open position.

Spencer blank plastic cartridges.

For quite some time, there were no replica Spencer rifles or carbines available at all. Original rim fire Spencer rifles and carbines were made to fire by installing newly manufactured center fire

42

The Civil War Reenactor's Blackpowder Guide

breech blocks which accommodated use of specially made ".56-50" brass (usually cut down from .50-70).

Spencer magazine follower partially withdrawn from the rifle.

However, in the last several years, newly manufactured replicas of the Spencer rifle and carbine have appeared in the marketplace. These replicas employ a similar type of center fire breech block and also employ the same center fire" .56-50" cartridge case. As no commercial ammunition is available for these, casting one's own bullets and loading one's own ammunition is the only way to fire one of these replicas "live".

Similarly, one must also load his or her own blank ammunition, but plastic blank cartridge hulls (similar to those used in the Henry rifle) make it relatively simple. These plastic hulls, available from several sources, are the proper size and shape of a live round and have a round primer hole at the base end. After filling the case with FFFG black powder, a shotgun primer is then seated in the primer hole and you are ready to go. Remember that the plastic cases, similar to those for the Henry, are designed for one time use and should be left on the field after being ejected from the rifle. *Remember that care should be taken in loading these cartridges in the Spencer's tubular magazine as the nose of each cartridge rests on the primer of the one ahead of it.*

The Spencer is cleared in similar fashion to the Henry, by lowering the trigger guard all the way and checking the chamber and the magazine tube for any ammunition. Loading the Spencer first entails removing the magazine follower from the rifle, by turning the follower base, located in the butt of the rifle clockwise and pulling the follower completely out of the gun. Holding the arm either level or at a slight angle with the muzzle down, cartridges may be loaded one at a time, nose first into the tubular magazine which runs through the stock of the gun. Once seven cartridges are loaded, the magazine follower is replaced and the Spencer is now ready to go. One need only lower the trigger guard all the way down, which opens the breech and then raise it, which chambers a round making it ready to fire. The hammer, as in the originals, must be cocked by hand. While using the Spencer rifle or carbine, be sure to follow all of the same basic safety rules as discussed previously.

Cleaning procedures are similar to those used for the Henry rifle. Remember that the internal parts of the breech must be cleaned with pipe cleaners and cotton swabs. It's usually wise to go back over the Spencer at least a couple of times to be sure that all the black powder fouling has been removed.

The Civil War Reenactor's Blackpowder Guide

Blank metallic cartridge firing replica revolvers

While some may consider these pieces to be firearm farberware, they aren't in the category of designer sunglasses or modern sneakers on the field. In fact, they will pass the "ten foot" rule except to the practiced eye. While certainly not acceptable to the purist, these pieces are useful to the occasional reenactor with limited time for cleaning and they have also proven helpful to mounted reenactors who need just a few shots a month to keep their horses trained to gunfire.

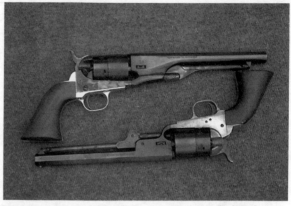

Blank metallic cartridge firing revolvers are designed to resemble the Colt 1860 Army (top) and 1851 Navy (bottom).

9 mm blank cartridge, live (right) and expended (left).

There are two models available which represent the Colt 1860 Army and 1851 Navy. Both are used with a metallic 9 millimeter blank cartridge which is crimped at the front and, similar to those for the Henry and Spencer rifles, are designed for one time use and then discarded. These revolvers are designed for blank firing only and cannot fire live ammunition. The cylinder, while chambered to accept the blank cartridge in the rear, is constricted in size in the middle area and then bored at an offset angle in the forward end so that it cannot possibly fire a live charge. Similarly, the revolver barrel is plugged at the end so that no projectile can be used and grooved on the bottom under the loading lever to allow the gases from the blank cartridge to vent.

Safety procedures are the same as for any other firearm. Before handling, the revolver must be cleared as follows: Point the revolver straight up in the air, place the hammer in the half cock position and rotate the cylinder to check that all six

Blank cartridge partly inserted in revolver.

The Civil War Reenactor's Blackpowder Guide

chambers are empty before further handling.

Loading the revolver is accomplished by sliding each cartridge through an expanded cap channel, enlarged to accept the blank cartridge, in the right side of the frame and into each firing successive chamber as the cylinder is rotated. *This revolver is <u>not equipped with safety pins between the chambers</u> and therefore must always be carried <u>with the hammer down over an empty chamber!</u>* After firing, the empties are removed by pushing them out from the front of the cylinder with a cleaning rod or other device.

Cleaning procedures for these pieces are similar to those for all regular percussion revolvers excepting that there are no nipples involved. Remember though, that flash powder, which is mildly corrosive, is used in the blank cartridges and therefore field stripping and cleaning should be done promptly.

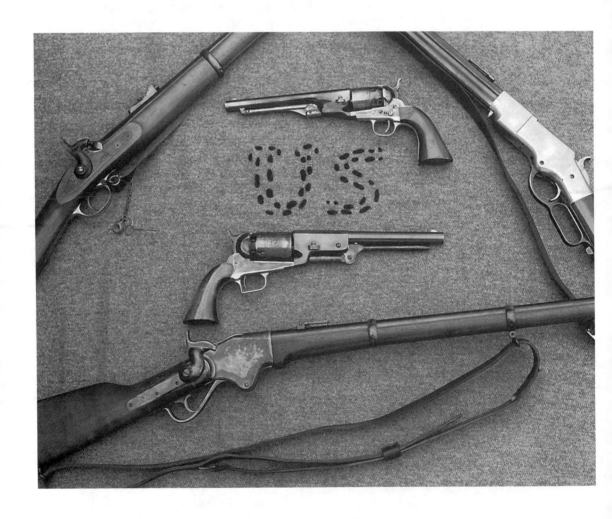

The Civil War Reenactor's Blackpowder Guide

Chapter 5 Notes

(1) Norm Flayderman, *Guide to Antique American Arms and their values 6th Edition,* (Northbrook, IL, DBI Books, 1994), 268.

(2) John D. McCauley, *Civil War Breech loading Rifles*, (Lincoln, RI, Andrew Mowbray, 1987), 42.

(3) John D. McCauley, *Carbines of the Civil War 1861 - 1865,* (Union City, TN, Pioneer Press, P.O. 1981), 32.

(4) Roy M. Marcot, *Spencer Repeating Firearms,* (Livonia, NY, R & R Books, 1983), 50; John D. McCauley, *Civil War Breech loading Rifles*, (Lincoln, RI, Andrew Mowbray, 1987), 108.

(5) Roy M. Marcot, *Spencer Repeating Firearms,* (Livonia, NY, R & R Books, 1983), 66, 70, 72; John D. McCauley, *Carbines of the Civil War 1861 - 1865,* (Union City, TN, Pioneer Press, P.O. 1981), 11, 12.

The Civil War Reenactor's Blackpowder Guide

Appendix 1 - Nipple Grid for Civil War replica black powder firearms

MODEL	MANUFACTURER	IMPORTER/MARKETER	NIPPLE DIAMETER & THREAD
Enfield rifle & musketoon	Gibbs Rifle (Post 1986)	Navy Arms	5/16" x 20 TPI
Enfield rifle & musketoon	Parker-Hale (Pre 1986)	Various	5/16" x 18 TPI
Enfield rifle & musketoon	Euroarms	Dixie	5/16" x 20 TPI
Enfield rifle & musketoon	Euroarms	Euroarms of America	8mm x 1.25mm
Enfield rifle	Armi-Sport	Taylor & Co	8mm x 1mm
1841 Mississippi rifle	Euroarms	Dixie	5/16" x 24 TPI
1841 Mississippi rifle	Euroarms	Euroarms of America	8mm x 1mm
1842 Musket .69 cal smoothbore	Armisport	Taylor & Co	8mm x 1mm
1842 Musket .69 cal Rifled Musket	Armisport	Taylor & Co	8mm x 1mm
1855 U.S. Rifle	Armi-Sport	Taylor & Co	8mm x 1mm
1861 Colt rifle	Colt	Chattahoochee Black Powder Arms	5/16" x 24 TPI
1861 Springfield	Miroku	Dixie	8mm x 1mm

The Civil War Reenactor's Blackpowder Guide

Appendix 1 - Nipple Grid for Civil War replica black powder firearms

MODEL	MANUFACTURER	IMPORTER/MARKETER	NIPPLE DIAMETER & THREAD
1861 Springfield	Euroarms	Euroarms of America	8mm x 1mm
1861 Springfield	Armi-Sport	Taylor & Co	8mm x 1mm
1863 Springfield	Miroku	Dixie	8mm x 1mm
1863 Zouave	Armi-Sport	Dixie and Taylor & Co	8mm x 1mm
1863 Zouave	Euroarms	Dixie & Euroarms of America	8mm x 1mm
J.P. Murray carbine	Euroarms	Dixie	5/16" x 24 TPI
J.P. Murray carbine	Euroarms	Euroarms of America	8mm x 1mm
Richmond musket	Euroarms	Euroarms & Dixie	8mm x 1mm
Richmond musket	Armi-Sport	Taylor & Co	8mm x 1mm
Cook & Brother carbine	Euroarms	Dixie	5/16" x 20 TPI
Cook & Brother carbine	Euroarms	Euroarms of America	8mm x 1.25mm
Sharps Carbine	IAB	Dixie	5/16" x 20 TPI

The Civil War Reenactor's Blackpowder Guide

Appendix 1 - Nipple Grid for Civil War replica black powder firearms

MODEL	MANUFACTURER	IMPORTER/MARKETER	NIPPLE DIAMETER & THREAD
Sharps Carbine	Armi San Marco	Dixie (Early 1990's)	5/16" x 20 TPI
Sharps Carbine & Rifle	Pedersoli	Dixie	5/16" x 24 TPI
Sharps Carbine & Rifle	Armi-Sport	Taylor & Co	8mm x 1mm
Smith Carbine	Pietta	Navy	5/16" x 24 TPI
1847 Walker	San Marco	Dixie	1/4" x 28 TPI
1847 Walker	Uberti	Dixie	6mm x .9mm
1848 Baby Dragoon	San Marco	Dixie	5.5mm x .9 mm
1848 Baby Dragoon	Uberti	Dixie	5.5mm x .9mm
New Model Pocket Remington	Italy	CVA	5.5mm x .9mm
Dragoon (all models)	Uberti	Dixie	6mm x .9mm
1849 Pocket	Uberti	Dixie	5.5mm x .9mm
1851 "Yank" (Navy Arms)	Pietta	Navy	6mm x .75mm

The Civil War Reenactor's Blackpowder Guide

Appendix 1 - Nipple Grid for Civil War replica black powder firearms

MODEL	MANUFACTURER	IMPORTER/MARKETER	NIPPLE DIAMETER & THREAD
1851 Navy (Dixie Gun Works)	"Italy"	Dixie	6mm x .75mm
1851 Navy brass frame (Dixie)	"Italy"	Dixie	6mm x .75mm
1851 Navy	Uberti	Dixie	5.5mm x .9mm
1851 Navy	Euroarms	Euroarms of America	12 x 28 TPI (SAE)
"Reb" 1851 Navy (Navy Arms)	Pietta	Navy	6mm x .75mm
"Reb" 1851 Navy	Euroarms	Euroarms of America	12 x 28 TPI (SAE)
1858 Remington	Euroarms	Dixie & Euroarms of America	6mm x .75mm
Remington Navy	Pietta	Dixie	6mm x .75mm
Remington Navy	Euroarms	Euroarms of America	6mm x .75mm
1858 Remington	Uberti	Dixie	5.5mm x .9mm
Remington Navy	Uberti	Dixie	5.5mm x .9mm
1858 Remington	Pietta	Navy	6mm x .75mm

The Civil War Reenactor's Blackpowder Guide

Appendix 1 - Nipple Grid for Civil War replica black powder firearms

MODEL	MANUFACTURER	IMPORTER/MARKETER	NIPPLE DIAMETER & THREAD
1860 Army	Euroarms	Euroarms of America	12 x 28 TPI (SAE)
1860 Army	Pietta	Dixie	6mm x .75mm
1860 Army	Uberti	Dixie	5.5mm x .9mm
1860 Army "Sheriff"	Pietta	Navy	6mm x .75mm
1860 Army	Pietta	Navy	6mm x .75mm
1861 Navy	Uberti	Dixie	5.5mm x .9mm
1862 Police	Uberti	Dixie	5.5mm x .9mm
Leech & Rigdon	Uberti	Dixie	5.5mm x .9mm
LeMat	Pietta	Navy	6mm x .75 mm
Spiller & Burr	Pietta	Dixie & Euroarms of America	6mm x .75mm
Rogers & Spencer	Euroarms	Dixie	6mm x .75mm
Old Army	Ruger	Ruger	12 x 24 TPI (SAE)

The Civil War Reenactor's Blackpowder Guide

Appendix 1 - Nipple Grid for Civil War replica black powder firearms

MODEL	MANUFACTURER	IMPORTER/MARKETER	NIPPLE DIAMETER & THREAD
MISCELLANEOUS ARMS			
1816 Percussion Conversion Musket	Pedersoli	Dixie	5/16 x 24
1842 .69 cal. smoothbore musket		Dixie	8mm x 1 mm
Maynard Carbine	Harpers Ferry Arms Company		5/16 x 24 TPI

IMPORTANT NOTE

While a great deal of research went into preparation of this nipple grid, it should be noted that it has been found through checking of sutlers' and dealers' inventory, that manufacturers sometimes do vary the nipple size in their percussion firearms from their published specification.

If any doubt exists about the size or thread of a nipple, use a thread gauge to determine the actual size and thread before attempting to install a replacement nipple!

The Civil War Reenactor's Blackpowder Guide

Appendix 2   Blackpowder Substitutes

There have been several attempts, some successful and others less so, to duplicate the propellant properties of black powder while reducing or eliminating some of the less desirable elements, such as corrosion, fouling and so forth. Each of these products has a limited application in the reenactment hobby and the primary focus of the discussion will therefore be on each product's usefulness in firing blank rounds.

Pyrodex Manufactured by Hodgdon Powder Company, Pyrodex is designed as a volume for volume equivalent for black powder in muzzle loading firearms. Its primary advantage is that Pyrodex's greater bulk and lighter weight makes a pound of it go further - up to 30% according to the company. The company also claims that fouling is considerably reduced.

The primary disadvantage of Pyrodex for blank musket loads is that uncompressed, it does not perform well. In fact, the company recommends that the ball (for live fire) "be seated **firmly** on the powder" (quoted from Pyrodex instructional brochure). This obviously limits Pyrodex's utility for musket or carbine blank loads, making it useful only to the reenactor who uses a revolver where loads are compressed.

The secondary disadvantage of Pyrodex is that it is about as corrosive as black powder so there will be no time saving in cleanup.

Black Canyon Manufactured by Legend Products. Advertised as a direct black powder replacement on a weight for weight basis, Black Canyon's primary advantage is that it is non-corrosive. Unfortunately, for the reenactor, the disadvantages far outweigh the advantages.

Similar to Pyrodex, Black Canyon must be compressed for the best results, again limiting its use to revolvers. Black Canyon has been observed on firing of blank revolver loads to project smoke and hot gasses a bit further from the muzzle than black powder, so care should be taken in close quarters.

The large granule size makes loading one's revolver more difficult. The only flask spout capable of handling Black Canyon's oversize powder granules is that for a musket flask and even that large a spout feeds the large granules with some difficulty. So the only real solution if one is determined to use Black Canyon is to make up paper cartridges in the prescribed charges and load your revolver using them. Be sure to use plain white paper as any chemically treated paper such as computer paper will react with Black Canyon if the cartridge is left unused for any extended period, usually resulting in the granules caking together making the cartridge useless.

The Civil War Reenactor's Blackpowder Guide

Glossary

Bolster — That part of the musket which houses the nipple and transfers the flash into the breech.

Bolt stop or Cylinder bolt — Part of revolver which stops the cylinder to align each chamber with the barrel when it is cocked.

Breech Block — Part of breechloading rifle or carbine that moves to expose the breech area allowing it to be loaded from the breech as opposed to the muzzle.

Breech Plug — Part which screws into the barrel of a muzzleloading musket; usually contains the nipple bolster or flash hole.

Cleanout Screw — Screw in the bolster of the 1861 Springfield to be removed to clean the bolster and flash channel.

Cylinder — Revolves around the cylinder pin aligning a chamber with the barrel each time the revolver is cocked.

Flash Channel — Hollowed channel of any musket of carbine which allows the flash from the percussion cap to reach the main powder charge.

Hand — Part of the revolver which turns the cylinder as the revolver is cocked.

Jag — A cleaning tool that approximates rifle bore diameter.

Magnaflux — A type of X-ray used to examine steels and other metals to find internal flaws and cracks.

Safety Pin — A pin manufactured as a part of Colt style revolver cylinders that fits into the slot in the hammer, securing it between chambers and allowing the revolver to be safely carried fully loaded.

The Civil War Reenactor's Blackpowder Guide

TPI Indicates threads per inch of any threaded surface such as a screw or a nipple.

Timing Adjustment of internal revolver parts, usually the hand, allowing each chamber to align perfectly with the barrel when cocked.

Trigger Bolt Spring Spring which keeps tension on the revolver cylinder bolt so that is locks the cylinder in place and keeps pressure on the trigger allowing it to return to its normal position after firing.

Worm A musket cleaning tool with a corkscrew on the end; also called a wiper.

The Civil War Reenactor's Blackpowder Guide

Need extra copies of this book?

Is this a borrowed copy? None left at your favorite sutler? Like to give one as a gift? Would you like to have it autographed? If so, send the name of the person you'd like mentioned together with your check and this order form.

Please rush ____ copies of **The Civil War Reenactor's Blackpowder Guide**© at $12.95 per copy.
Please add $2.00 shipping & handling.
PA Residents please add 6% Sales Tax

Name_____

Number & Street_____

Town_____ State_____ ZIP_____

Send to: Rusty Musket Enterprises, P.O. Box 3574, Gettysburg, PA 17325

Dealer inquiries invited.